I AM
Good
and
YOU ARE
Loved

by
Dr. Dan Coflin

I am Good and You are Loved
ISBN: 978-0-9970643-2-2
Copyright © 2020 by
Dan Coflin
Coflin Family Publishing
orders@coflinfamilypublishing.com

Cover by: April Robinson, Graphic Artist
Text Design: Lisa Simpson
SimpsonProductions.net

Contents

Introduction

This book is all about spiritual birth, spiritual growth and living a life that is fruitful, rewarding and as Jesus said, "more abundant."

It seems that the people of our nation, today more than at any other time in our history, are uncertain and confused about God, who He is, what He is like and what He will or will not do. Unfortunately, the political policies of some liberal leaders have successfully removed from our educational system the study of the most important book mankind possesses. The very authority of the Bible, as the Word of God, is not only questioned but also ridiculed among our educated elite who see the scriptures as irrelevant for us today.

I know you have heard, as I have, people with absolutely no knowledge of the Bible, mock it as a book of fairy tales and fantasies, that is full of historical inaccuracies and proven scientific impossibilities. These same people cannot show from the Bible these supposed inaccuracies and contradictions they are certain exist. They only seek to prove their opinions by basing their claims on what they have heard someone else say and not by their own sincere research.

I realize that some people would argue that we couldn't know for certain if "the Truth" is contained in the Bible or some other written work of an almost endless number of different religions and philosophies of man. But I am certain that the truth about God, that is revealed through the Bible, is available to everyone who will throw away every preconceived idea and with a sincere heart listen to what the Bible teaches and let the Spirit of God bring whatever revelation is needed for him or her to not just believe but experience a new and wonderful life.

Chapter 1

WHY DOES MAN NEED A NEW LIFE?

For most of us the answer to this question is obvious. Man-kind is hurt, broken, tormented, full of guilt and shame, burdened down with sin and is sick, stressed, broke and in great need for someone to help. There is good news for all of us, and that good news is that God's greatest desire is for us to receive forgiveness, to be healed, delivered from the wounds and bondages of our past and brought into a new life—a life we have never experienced before; a life that is rich in love and free from fear.

For us to understand the kind of life God wants us to have and enjoy, we must go back to the record of God's original plan for man.

God designed man to be His representative on the earth. Man was made to be just a little lower than God* (Psalm 8:5)

---

*In many translations Psalm 8:5 says, "made him a little lower than the angels," but the Hebrew word here is *elohiym* and is translated 2,346 times as God and only one time as angels.

and was made in God's image to have authority and dominion over all of God's creation (Genesis 1:26-28).

As we read in the Book of Genesis, chapter 2, we discover that God placed man into a garden. This was not just any garden. It was indeed a paradise with every possible provision. The beauty and comfort afforded man in this garden can only be imagined. If we look at the most breathtaking views of our day and imagine these places with every tree, every plant, every flower perfectly formed with no flaws or imperfections, no weeds or destructive insects, but only flawless beauty, we could only get a glimpse of the wondrous perfection of this place God made for man. Even beyond its beauty and abundance was an even greater reality. There was no death in that place. There was no fear, lack, sickness or any such thing because this place was made for man but was inhabited by God. Everything in this environment was perfect. This was God's idea for man. This was God's will, His plan and His desire.

God created this planet and this garden for man in all of its perfection, and then handed over the responsibility of running this place to man. God had given man authority and dominion. Now man is in charge. To prepare man for this responsibility, God gave him some instructions to follow. God gave man the truth about how things in God's creation operate. God gave man an understanding of laws that govern the way things function.

We all recognize certain physical laws that govern this physical universe. An example of one of these laws is gravity. If you drop something out of your pocket or if you throw a ball into the air, it will fall to the ground because the law of gravity is at work.

Just as there are physical laws, there are also spiritual laws. An example of one of the spiritual laws God gave to man is recorded in Genesis, chapter 2:

"But of the tree of the knowledge of good and evil you shall not eat, for in the day that you eat of it you shall surely die."

Genesis 2:17 NKJV

Our English Bible is translated from the Hebrew language here in the Book of Genesis. This verse in Hebrew would read, in modern English, more like this: **"In the day you eat of it you shall die, and in dying you shall surely die."**

Sadly, the man, Adam, ate of this forbidden tree, and yet we see in the scriptures that he continued to live for many years. The spiritual law that Adam set in motion by his disobedience was the law of sin and death.

We tend to think of death as cessation of life, but death also means separation. When someone dies, the real person (their personality, character, thoughts, etc.) leaves the physical body they once lived in. Their body is dead; that is, it ceases to live because the life that once inhabited that physical body has left. The real person has moved out and is no longer there. There is a separation of the real person from their physical body.

The day the man Adam sinned by disobeying God's command, the law of sin and death went into effect. That day Adam died (was separated from God) spiritually, and as a result of his spiritual death, he would eventually die physically ("in dying you shall surely die").

You see, the Bible explains to us that we are a three-part being: spirit, soul and body. We were made in the image and likeness of God (Father, Son and Holy Spirit). The Bible tells us: **"God is a Spirit: and they that worship him must worship him in spirit and in truth"** (John 4:24).

Mankind is a spiritual being who lives in a physical body. The Bible explains man as a three-part being:

"And the very God of peace sanctify you wholly; and I pray God your whole spirit and soul and body be preserved blameless unto the coming of our Lord Jesus Christ."
1 Thessalonians 5:23

The most obvious part of man is his physical body. It is the part he looks at in the mirror every day. It is by his physical body that he relates to this physical world in which he lives.

The soul of man is described as his mind, will and emotions. It is where he thinks, reasons, debates and comes to conclusions and understandings of the situations that surround him. Man takes the facts he receives from his senses and processes them according to his understanding and makes decisions.

The spirit of man is less obvious. The spirit of man is how he relates to God. Man's spirit is described in the Book of Proverbs as the "candle," or more accurately, the "lamp" of the Lord.

"The spirit of man is the candle of the Lord, searching all the inward parts of the belly."
Proverbs 20:27

Then again, in the Book of Psalms we have the picture of an oil lamp with its wick unlit. This is the condition of man's spirit without God in his life. When the Spirit of God enters the spirit of man, He "lights his lamp."

"For You will light my lamp [candle]; the Lord my God will enlighten my darkness."

Psalm 18:28 NKJV

The day the man Adam disobeyed God, he died spiritually; that is, his spirit man went dark. It was as if his spirit was like a candle, and when he decided to disobey God, someone blew out the flame and Adam's spirit went dark.

This act of disobedience ushered in the results God had warned him about. Death had entered man's world. Man's spiritual death (separation from God) would eventually lead to his physical death. The spiritual law of sin that results in death had entered, not only Adam's body, but also all of the creation God had given Adam dominion over. Everything around him began to die. Creation itself was brought under the curse of sin and its resulting death. Adam had opened a door he could not shut.

To help us understand how this act of disobedience affected, not only Adam, but also all the things God had given Adam authority over, let's look at this example.

If you are given a piece of property with a lovely yard, a beautiful house and a bountifully producing garden, you then become responsible for that piece of property and what happens to it. If you choose to not do the things that are necessary to maintain the physical condition of that house and property, you must live with the outcome. If you refuse to keep paint on the house and fence, you never cut the grass or repair the roof and you don't water and weed the garden, it will not take very long for everything to begin to fail. If your roof leaks and water gets into your house so that mold and mildew take over and weeds and bugs invade your garden so that the tomatoes and squash are choked out by the weeds and eaten by the bugs, you cannot blame the previous owner for the current condition of the property.

Neither would it be lawful for the previous owner to see the terrible condition that now exists and just show up and take charge, fixing what was wrong even though he may have the know-how and resources to do so.

No, you have been given the responsibility of caring for that place, and what you choose to do will determine the outcome. You cannot blame the previous owner for the current condition of things, even if he was the one who cleared the land, built the house and planted the garden, because even though he did those things, he gave it to you.

God's greatest desire for man was clearly seen in the environment God had made for man. This perfect place filled with every joy and blessing was possible because of God's presence there. When Adam sinned, his spiritual separation from God's presence was exemplified by his being banished from the garden.

"Therefore the Lord God sent him forth from the garden of Eden . . . So he drove out the man; and he placed at the east of the garden of Eden Cherubims, and a flaming sword which turned every way, to keep the way of the tree of life."
Genesis 3:23,24

Man could no longer enjoy or partake of God's presence (the tree of life), and all of the blessings and benefits God desired for man were forfeited. Man had become separated from God because of his sin. Man no longer had the benefit of God ruling in his life. Instead man became enslaved to his disobedience. Man could not cease from sinning, and the result of his sin was always death. The law of sin and death was in full swing. The curse sin ushered in filled all the earth. Sickness, disease, poverty, lack, fear, death—all of the things forbidden in God's presence ruled in God's absence in man's life.

The following scriptures reveal these truths:

"Behold, the Lord's hand is not shortened, that it cannot save; neither his ear heavy, that it cannot hear: but your iniquities have separated between you and your God, and your sins have hid his face from you, that he will not hear."

Isaiah 59:1,2

"Do you not know that to whom you yield yourselves as slaves to obey, you are slaves of the one whom you obey, whether of sin leading to death, or of obedience leading to righteousness?"

Romans 6:16 MEV

"Then when lust has conceived, it brings forth sin; and sin, when it is finished, brings forth death."

James. 1:15 JUB

Adam and all of his descendants became subject to the spiritual law of sin and death. Once sin occurred, death entered; and the law of sin and death produced in this world what would be later known as the "curse of the law." This curse is described in the Book of Leviticus, chapter 26, and the Book of Deuteronomy, chapter 28. These chapters describe the awful results for anyone who does not obey every commandment, every statute and every word of God. I will just briefly mention a few of these things: sickness, blindness, deafness, fear, torment, insanity, poverty, loss of security, loss of family, death, every imaginable disease, addiction, slavery, drought, pestilence and so forth.

This terrible list of curses, resulting from man's sin, may give people the wrong idea about God. So often I hear people say, "If God is so good, how could He let such terrible things happen to people?" The problem with this statement is the misconception people have that God is in control of everything that happens in the earth, but that is just not true.

Too often I hear good intentioned Christians say, "Well, we might not understand why now (whatever terrible tragedy they are referring to), but we know God is in control and He knows best; one day we might understand." The problem with that kind of statement is that it is based on ignorance of the character of God and ignorance of the Word of God.

Chapter 2

WHO'S IN CHARGE ANYWAY?

First of all, God gave man dominion and authority over all of His creation. Man is still in charge and responsible for what happens in the earth. Unfortunately, when man sinned, he lost the character and benevolent nature of God and took upon himself an evil and rebellious sin nature. This is evident in the fact that the smallest child does not need to be taught to do wrong; he must be taught to do what is right. Why? It is in his very nature to do wrong and be rebellious.

The perfect image of God in man was displaced with a rebellious sin nature the moment Adam chose to disobey God and allow the law of sin and death to take effect. Man is no longer carrying the image and nature of God, which is love, compassion, unselfishness, integrity, holiness, etc., but a corrupt nature based on selfishness, lust, greed, hate, rebellion, etc. So, the driving force behind man becomes his insatiable desire for power, wealth and sensual pleasure.

Man's guilty conscience produces in him a desire to be rid of the remembrance of God's commandments, and so tyrants and demagogues through the centuries have banned the Bible and burned churches trying to relieve themselves of the reminders of their sin. Even today when a government or an authoritative head of an organization bans prayer or Bible reading on its premises, they are acting on their God-given authority to say, "God, You are not welcome here in this part of the earth where I have dominion," and God honors that. But, as soon as some tragedy takes place, the mockers' cry is, "If God is good, why didn't He do something to stop this?" The sad truth is, God was not allowed to interfere.

I know some will say that God is in control of everything and so everything happens according to His will. There is a major problem with this kind of thinking. God has already made His will quite plain. The Ten Commandments recorded in Exodus 20 reveal that idolatry, adultery, murder and lying are not God's will. These things are forbidden by God, and yet these are common practices in the everyday life of millions of people.

We also have God's intention for all people described in the Book of 2 Peter where God's will is plainly declared. God is not willing that anyone would perish, but that all would come to repentance and be restored to God's presence (2 Peter 3:9).

Here we see that it is not God's will for any person to perish (come to ruin or destruction), and yet we witness multitudes perishing daily. So, quite obviously the will of God is not always done. God is not in control of all things that happen in the earth.

Because God gets the blame for the curse of man's sin in the earth (babies dying of disease or starvation, etc.), many people cannot understand the love of God. The Bible shows us that the greatest description of God's character is love.

> **"Beloved, let us love one another, for love is of God; and everyone who loves is born of God and knows God. He who does not love does not know God, for God is love."**
>
> **1 John. 4:7,8 NKJV**

As any parent would be distressed because of a wayward child, God weeps over the sin of man and the destruction it causes him.

> **"Do I take any pleasure in the death of the wicked?" This is the declaration of the Lord GOD. "Instead, don't I take pleasure when he turns from his ways and lives?"**
>
> **Ezekiel 18:23 CSB**

> **"I call heaven and earth to record this day against you, that I have set before you life and death, blessing and cursing: therefore choose life, that both [you] and [your] seed may live."**
>
> **Deuteronomy 30:19**

We see the tender love and compassion of God poured out even on those who have been His enemies. When judgment fell on the wicked nation of Moab, God said:

"Therefore I will wail for Moab, even for all Moab will I cry out; I will moan for the men of Kirheres. More than the weeping for Jazer I will weep for you. . . ."
Jeremiah 48:31, 32 NASB

God is not ignoring man's troubles and suffering. He is saddened by the awful results of man's choices.

On more than one occasion, my wife and I have met with women who shared with us their experience of sexual abuse from a very early age. These women, who love God and want to trust Him with their lives and families, have struggled with their experience of calling out to God as a young child and praying for the abuse to stop and it never did. They could not understand how a loving God could let such a terrible violation happen year after year to an innocent child.

These same women blamed themselves, thinking that something must be wrong with them for God to let this happen. Deep down, they were angry with God because all their lives they were told that "nothing can happen to you except God allows it and that someday the pain of it will be worthwhile because God knows what is best." These empty words could not bring any peace to these women because there was no truth to them. What they needed to hear was that God wept for them, and His heart broke because of their pain and heartache.

Is God big enough and strong enough to make right what is wrong, stop injustices and protect and provide for the innocent? The answer is obviously yes, but God will not violate the authority He gave to man to choose.

Because God's very nature is love and His desire is to see man live free from the effects of sin and the curse it produced,

He gave man a system to live by. This system would give God access to work in man's behalf and restore to him the blessings of God without violating the authority God gave to man. This would not be God's perfect or final remedy for man, but it was a necessary step.

This idea may seem strange to many who only see God as Almighty and Powerful and Sovereign, always accomplishing His will. There is no doubt that God is all-powerful and mighty and could have destroyed man for his sin and disobedience. God could have flooded the earth and not saved Noah and his family. If you only consider the power and ability God has, then there is nothing that He cannot do or accomplish.

There are those who only see God's sovereignty and power, but they must not be ignorant of God's lovingkindness and tender mercies. God's character is revealed through His love, not His power. God is not a destroyer, but a restorer. He is slow to anger and full of mercy. God's system was the beginning of His eternal plan to fully restore man to everything he lost in the garden.

God's temporary remedy for man's sin is found in the pages of the Old Testament. As soon as Adam sinned, he was put out from the presence of God but not before God clothed Adam's nakedness with the skins of animals. This was the beginning of God's redemptive work to restore to man all man had lost because of his sin. I do not believe God simply manufactured animal skins, but killed the animals to cover man's sin.

The Bible declares, **"Without shedding of blood there is no remission** [of sin]**" (Hebrews 9:22 NKJV).** Because the physical body cannot survive without blood, the shedding of blood is evidence that death has occurred. God shed the blood of the animals to bring a temporary satisfaction to His required judgment for sin, which is death. God then covered man's physical nakedness with the skins of animals, but He covered the sin of man with the blood of the animals.

Adam had attempted to cover his own nakedness by sewing fig leaves together. Man always tries to devise his own system apart from God, which is the essence of religion (man's attempts to please God). Man's efforts could not eliminate his guilt. His own works could not cover his nakedness. No wonder it was a fig tree that Jesus cursed for it only had leaves, no real fruit.

Man's best efforts to make himself acceptable to God and cover his sin by his own works is nothing more than foolishness in God's eyes. The Bible describes man's efforts to make himself righteous (right before God) as "filthy rags." No matter how much "good" someone might accomplish, they can never erase past sin or change their nature by their own will or desire. That is why Jesus said the way into God's family is not attained by your family heritage, by the will of another or by your own efforts, but only by being born of the Spirit (John 1:13).

This example of covering man's sin with blood would be later explained in great detail when God gave Moses the Law. This system of sacrifices and laws was based on blessings to those who obeyed the commands of God and curses to those who disobeyed and rebelled. The law of God was uncompromising. It required no less than perfect obedience and conformity without exception.

Anytime there was a violation of the law, a blood sacrifice was required, and the ugly results of man's sin was exposed by the death of another. An animal was brought before the priest and the guilty person laid his hands on the head of the animal, symbolically transferring his sin to the animal. Then the animal's throat was slit, and its blood was poured out. Proof that death had occurred was the blood upon the altar, and the judgment that rightfully belonged to the one who sinned was placed on the substitute instead.

Even after the sacrifice was made, the man who sinned was still guilty; however, the judgment God required was fulfilled. Man could, once again, have a relationship with God and walk in God's blessings, as long as he continued to obey God's commandments and bring the necessary sacrifices to the priests when he failed. This process was burdensome and always reminded man of his sin and shortcomings.

Man was still battling his sinful nature and fleshly desires. His constant failures and the hardships they brought into his life caused him to live in despair. But when man followed the laws of God, he could walk in God's blessings and forgiveness, and God's presence would bring to man victory over his enemies and success in all he purposed in his heart to do.

There were times when godly kings would rule over the people. King David and Solomon, Hezekiah and Josiah were just a few of the righteous kings who ruled in Israel and Judah. During the reigns of these righteous kings, the nation was blessed because the people were required to reject the many false gods of the surrounding nations and worship Jehovah, the one true God. Great care was given to keep all of the commandments and laws of sacrifice the Word of God required. It was during these times that God worked great and mighty wonders to protect and deliver His covenant people (those who kept and obeyed His laws).

But soon an ungodly king would arise who would lead the nation into the worship of false gods and ungodly practices that would result in the curse (the result of man's sin) and bring destruction and great trouble into the lives of the people. This cycle of blessing and rebellion, disaster and repentance occurred over and over again throughout the centuries.

Chapter 3

THE FALL OF LUCIFER

The practice of animal sacrifices to cover man's sin was never the final plan of God for man. The blood of the animals could never remove man's guilt or restore to man everything he lost when Adam sinned. The Book of Galatians shows us that **"...the law was our schoolmaster to bring us unto Christ, that we might be justified by faith" (Galatians 3:24).**

The word "justified" means to be made righteous or to bring into right standing with God. To be justified or made right indicates far more than covering over the guilt of man's sin with the blood of an animal. The death of an animal could never deal with the heart or nature of man to cleanse him from his sin. The sentence of death that was required by God's righteous judgment may have been placed on the substitute (the animal) instead of on the man, but the man was still guilty of sin; and he was still not righteous before God because the very nature of man was still sinful.

From the very beginning God had a solution for man's sin and guilt and evil nature. A remedy that would not just cover

over man's sin, but totally remove his guilt and restore him to a righteous relationship with God just as if he had never sinned in the first place.

In the Book of Genesis, God declared to the serpent (the devil), **"And I will put enmity between you and the woman, and between your seed and her Seed; He shall bruise your head, and you shall bruise His heel" (Genesis 3:15 NKJV).**

This is the first prophecy God gives to us that One would come who would be the "seed of the woman" and would accomplish the work of crushing or destroying the serpent (the devil).

Let's first take a look at the "serpent" (the devil) and discover who he is, what he does and why his "head" (authority) needed to be "bruised" or crushed.

In the Book of Revelation, we see war in heaven.

"And there was war in heaven: Michael and his angels fought against the dragon; and the dragon fought and his angels, and prevailed not; neither was their place found any more in heaven. And the great dragon was cast out, that old serpent, called the Devil, and Satan, which [deceived] the whole world: he was cast out into the earth, and his angels were cast out with him."

Revelation 12:7-9

Here we find the serpent, who is called the devil and Satan, fighting with his angels against the angels of God.

Who is the devil, and where did he come from?

When Jesus was debating with the religious leaders, there was an argument over "who their father was." Jesus then plainly tells them, "[You] **are of your father the devil, and the lusts of your father** [you] **will do. He was a murderer from the beginning, and abode not in the truth, because there is no truth in him . . ."** (John 8:44). Here we discover several things about the devil.

First, he was a "murderer from the beginning." This is in reference to the first murder recorded in the Bible. In the Book of Genesis, we see the eldest son of Adam and Eve (Cain) killing his brother Abel (Genesis 4:8). Jesus is showing us that the man Cain actually killed his brother, but the reason he did was because he was acting like his father, the devil. The spirit of hate and murder with the nature that kills and destroys was working in Cain when he rose up and slew his brother. In 1 John 3:12 it tells us not to be like Cain: **"Not as Cain, who was of that wicked one, and slew his brother. . . ."**

Secondly, Jesus shows us that the devil did not "abide in the truth." That means there was a time when he was in the truth, but he did not remain there. You see, God created all things and everything God created was good. The names Satan and the devil have very similar meanings. Satan means "accuser" and devil means "traducer" or false accuser, slanderer. These names describe the character or nature of this spirit.

This wicked one was originally created as an anointed Cherub. The Bible identifies the "cherubim" as those angelic beings who minister about the throne of God. Most every time cherubim are mentioned, we see the glory of God, the throne of God or the presence of God close by (Genesis 3:24; Ezekiel 28:14). In the Book of Ezekiel, there is one who is described as the anointed cherub who was on the holy mountain of God and was perfect until iniquity (sin, impurity) was found in him.

"You were the anointed cherub that covers, and I set you there; you were upon the holy mountain of God . . . You were perfect in your ways from the day that you were created, until iniquity was found in you."
Ezekiel 28:14,15 MEV

So, there was a time in God's creation when everything was perfect, and everything operated according to the will of God. But there came a time when one of these anointed cherubs rebelled against God and was cast out of God's presence, and along with him, some of the angels who followed his leadership. This was the reason for the chaotic conditions we see in the earth as is described in Genesis 1:2: **"And the earth was without form, and void; and darkness was upon the face of the deep. . . ."**

This rebellion had devastating effects. In the Book of Isaiah, we are told:

"For thus saith the LORD that created the heavens; God himself that formed the earth and made it; he [has] established it, he created it not in vain, he formed it to be inhabited: I am the LORD; and there is none else."
Isaiah 45:18

The prophet Isaiah informs us that God did not create the earth "in vain," "dark" and "without form," which are the same words Genesis uses to describe the condition of the earth. The words "created it not in vain" in Isaiah and the words "without

THE FALL OF LUCIFER

form" in Genesis 1:2 are the same. The definition of these Hebrew words is as follows:

> **tohuw** – without form: meaning to lie waste, a desolation (of surface), that is a desert or figuratively worthless thing or in vain (*Strong's* #8414).

> **bohuw** – void: meaning to be empty; a vacuity that is superficially an undistinguishable ruin (*Strong's* #922).

> **choshek** – darkness: meaning the dark, literally darkness; figuratively misery, destruction, death, ignorance, sorrow, wickedness (*Strong's* #2822).

According to these definitions, the earth was a desolate ruin. It was a worthless place filled with misery, destruction and death. God did not create the earth in this condition. The earth was perfect until it was devastated by sin and rebellion brought into it by the fall of this cherub who came to be known as the devil or Satan.

The earth literally "became" without form and void—a very different condition than when God originally created it. I believe this simple explanation should end the typical debates between many scientists and creationists who argue over the age of the earth. Scientists can show that the age of a rock or fossil is millions of years old, while many creationists hold to a young earth idea that the Genesis account occurred just over 6,000 years ago. I would agree that the account we read about in the Book of Genesis happened just over 6,000 years ago, but this is a record of a re-creation, not the original work of God.

After God's re-creation of the earth, described in Genesis, chapter 1, we see God creating man in His own image. God placed man in this beautiful garden and gave him dominion over everything. One purpose God had for man in this garden was to "keep it" (Genesis 2:15). This means to hedge about, guard, protect. Obviously, there was something or someone Adam was supposed to "keep" out of the garden. God knew there would be an intruder to tempt man and destroy his life and God's creation.

It was only a short time until we see Satan, the tempter, coming to accuse God and tempt man to sin and disobey God.

God's desire for man has never been anything but good. In God's Kingdom everything is perfect. There is no sin, no curse, no fear or sorrow or any such thing. This is in such contrast to the working of Satan who, as is described in John 10:10, is the one who comes to "steal, kill and destroy." Satan's temptation began with the woman Eve when he challenges the Word of God by saying, **"You will not surely die" (Genesis 3:4 NKJV).** He then caused the woman to look at the forbidden tree in a different manner than what God had commanded.

> **"So when the woman saw that the tree was good for food, and that it was pleasant to the eyes, and a tree desirable to make one wise, she took of its fruit and ate. She also gave to her husband with her, and he ate."**
>
> **Genesis 3:6 NKJV**

This act of the first couple did not just make them guilty of a wrong. It caused them to become separated from God's holiness by sin and brought them under the dominion of the wicked one whom they chose to obey. God is the Father, the source, of everything that is good and perfect and just and holy. The devil, on the other hand, is the father, the source, of everything that is wicked and ungodly. Everywhere he rules we find death and destruction, poverty and disease, fear and torment. All of these things are characteristic of his kingdom of darkness.

It does not take much enlightenment to see the vast difference in the standard of living between the people of nations that are dominated by pagan ideas and have been under the control of witchcraft and other demonic activities and those of nations where there has been a strong Christian influence. Just a casual look at the United States, England and the Western European nations reveal a time in their history when powerful preaching of the Word of God produced mass repentance of the majority of the population. Entire nations were converted and lived their lives, as a people, and established laws, as a nation, according to the Word of God. These nations have enjoyed the blessings of God as described in the Bible.

Even though the people of these nations may not be embracing the things of God today, they still enjoy the benefits of those righteous believers from generations past, while those in nations with little Christian heritage have seldom enjoyed prosperity or liberty. But, even in those places where the darkness of paganism has prevailed, we see what happens when the gospel of Jesus Christ is introduced into a region. A good example is in regions of India where the English had much control for many years, bringing with them the gospel. This resulted in the conversion of many in those areas, and the people there enjoy a much greater standard of living and liberty than the rest of India because of the blessings of God.

Man's sin in the Garden of Eden placed him under the dominion of that wicked, rebellious spirit he obeyed. Man became like his father, disobedient to God and under the curse of sin and death. Man needed more than forgiveness. He needed a new nature. He needed to be changed at his very core in order to desire to please God and to once again possess the character and nature of God. Man needed to be "born again" into a new family where God is his Father.

This brings us to the first prophetic promise of One who would come and be man's Savior, One who would deliver him from the authority of the wicked one and usher man back into a right relationship with God.

Chapter 4

BORN OF A SEED

In Genesis, chapter 3, this prophetic word is declared. Speaking to the serpent, God says:

> **"And I will put enmity (hostility) between you and the woman, and between your seed and her Seed; He shall bruise your head, and you shall bruise His heel."**
>
> **Genesis 3:15 NKJV**

God promises the coming of One who would be called the "seed of the woman," and He would crush (bruise) the serpent's head and in the process the serpent would bruise His heel. Who is this "seed of the woman"?

There is an obvious contradiction to the biological process here for the birth of a baby. The seed (sperm), as we all know, is not carried by the woman, but by the man. But here there is a purposeful employment of this unusual term "seed of the woman." In God's design we find that every seed produces "after its kind."

**"And God said, Let the earth bring forth grass, the
herb yielding seed, and the fruit tree yielding fruit
after his kind, whose seed is in itself, upon the earth:
and it was so."**

Genesis 1:11

This design for everything to produce by a seed after its
kind is spoken over every living thing God created. Whether it
is the fish of the sea, the birds of the air, the animals of the field
or mankind, all will bring forth offspring just like themselves
from a seed.

In the Book of Genesis, chapter 4, we see children born to
Adam and Eve. These children were made after the image of
their father, Adam, for they were born of his seed. They were
born after Adam's sinful nature, for his seed produced them.
The following scriptures show that all of the children of Adam
were born into sin because Adam was sinful:

**"Wherefore, as by one man sin entered into the world,
and death by sin; and so death passed upon all men,
for that all have sinned."**

Romans 5:12

"For if by one man's offence death reigned by one . . . ."

Romans 5:17

**"Therefore as by the offence of one judgment came
upon all men to condemnation . . . For as by one
man's disobedience many were made sinners. . . ."**

Romans 5:18,19

**"For since by man came death . . . For as in Adam all
die. . . ."**

1 Corinthians 15:21,22

In these scriptures we see that all of Adam's children were just like him, because his seed produced them. Since every succeeding generation is produced the same way, all of mankind is born with a sinful nature and is under the curse of sin and death. It does not matter if you were born directly from Adam or a thousand generations later, you are still born into Adam's family, produced from his seed and born after his kind.

Man needed a way out of Adam's likeness and to be changed into God's likeness, but there was no way man could accomplish this on his own. He was born of Adam's seed, and there was no way for him to be unborn; however, God had a plan. God's plan was to totally redeem man and restore to him everything he had lost by his sin and rebellion. The promised "seed of the woman" would be a man, born of a woman, but this man would not be born of Adam's seed.

"And behold, you will conceive in your womb and bring forth a Son, and shall call his name JESUS. He will be great, and will be called the Son of the Highest. . . ."

Luke 1:31,32 NKJV

Then said Mary unto the angel, "How can this be, since I do not know a man?" And the angel answered and said to her, "*The* Holy Spirit will come upon you, and the power of the Highest will overshadow you; therefore, also, that Holy One who is to be born will be called the Son of God."

Luke 1:34,35 NKJV

"But when the fulness of the time was come, God sent forth his Son, made of a woman, made under the

law, to redeem them that were under the law, that we might receive the adoption of sons."

Galatians 4:4,5

Each of these scriptures refers to the Son of God being born of a woman. We know that woman was Mary; and when she asked the angel about becoming pregnant, the angel said that the Spirit of God would produce in her womb a child. This child would not have the sinful nature of Adam's descendants, but would be born in the image and likeness of God as Adam was before he sinned.

"And so it is written, The first man Adam was made a living soul; the last Adam was made a quickening [life giving] spirit. Howbeit that was not first which is spiritual, but that which is natural; and afterward that which is spiritual. The first man is of the earth, earthy: the second man is the Lord from heaven."

1 Corinthians 15:45-47

In this scripture we see Adam, whom God made in His image and placed him in the Garden of Eden, is called the "first" man. Jesus, in this scripture, is called the "second" man. We all know that there were literally millions of men born in the time frame between Adam's creation and Jesus' birth, so why is Jesus called the "second" man? The answer is really very simple. Adam was indeed created in God's image and likeness, but after Adam sinned, he no longer held that image and nature of God.

All of the children born to Adam and his descendants held Adam's sinful nature and not God's righteous nature. When Jesus was born, He was not born of Adam's descendants but of God Himself. Jesus was the second man to walk the earth in the

34

image and likeness of God. He was not sinful or separated from God but walked in perfect agreement with God, without sin as God intended all men to be.

In this same scripture we see Adam referred to as the first man and Jesus being referred to as the "last" Adam. Just as Adam was the source or fountainhead of the family of all mankind, Jesus was the last Adam, that is, the source or fountainhead of a family who would be born after His kind. The first man, Adam, was made of the earth and fathered children after the flesh. Jesus was from Heaven. He was the Son of God and would bring forth children who would be born of the Spirit as He was.

You Must Be Born Again

One night, a high-ranking leader in the government of Israel visited Jesus. His name was Nicodemus. He was a member of the Sanhedrin (the "supreme court" of Israel) and came to Jesus seeking some answers.

"Jesus answered and said unto him, Verily, verily, I say unto [you], Except a man be born again, he cannot see the kingdom of God."

John 3:3

Jesus' reply to Nicodemus was confusing to him so he asked Jesus: **"How can a man be born when he is old?"** (John 3:4).

The response Jesus gave to Nicodemus helps explain the spiritual birth: **"That which is born of the flesh is flesh; and that which is born of the Spirit is spirit"** (John 3:6).

We were all born of the flesh. Every one of us has a biological father. Our biological father is only able to give us physical life. Through our natural father, we were all "born of the flesh." Jesus told Nicodemus that he must be "born of the Spirit" to see the Kingdom of God.

According to the Word of God, everything produces from a seed. Biologically, we understand a child is conceived from the seed of man, and the result is a physical birth. In like manner, a spiritual birth must come from a spiritual seed.

As we discussed previously, man is a three-part being: spirit, soul and body. When a child is born into the world, he possesses all three parts of man (spirit, soul and body), but his spirit is not alive to the things of God. His nature is sinful, and he is governed by selfish needs with no understanding of God. This child will grow to adulthood and can live his entire life separated from God and enslaved by sin, for he has only been born of the flesh.

A person cannot change their nature by self-discipline or by the restrictions and discipline brought by another. You cannot educate or subjugate your nature to be anything other than sinful. People may successfully conform their behavior because of their own desires or that are forced on them by another, but at their core there is a rebellious and sensual nature that has been passed on to them by their father.

We have already seen that it takes physical seed to be born physically. We need to also understand that it takes spiritual seed to be born spiritually. Jesus told us what spiritual seed is: **"…the words that I speak unto you, they are spirit, and they are life" (John 6:63)**. To be "born of the Spirit," we must be born of the Word of God.

To help us understand what that means, let's look at the record of creation in the book of Genesis.

"And God said, Let there be light: and there was light ... And God said, Let there be a firmament in the midst of the waters . . . and it was so."

Genesis 1:3,6,7

We could continue verse after verse in this first chapter of Genesis and see God saying over and over again, "Let there be" and "there was." There are many scriptures in both the Old and New Testaments showing us that God created all things by His Word. God spoke into being all of creation.

"By the word of the LORD were the heavens made; and all the host of them by the breath of his mouth."

Psalm 33:6

"Through faith we understand that the worlds were framed by the word of God, so that things which are seen were not made of things which do appear."

Hebrews 11:3

There are many references to Jesus as the Word of God. In the gospel of John, it declares:

"In the beginning was the Word, and the Word was with God, and the Word was God. The same was in the beginning with God. All things were made by him; and without him was not any thing made that was made."

John 1:1-3

"And the Word was made flesh, and dwelt among us, (and we beheld his glory, the glory as of the only begotten of the Father,) full of grace and truth."

John 1:14

"His name is called The Word of God."

Revelation 19:13 NKJV

When the angel Gabriel visited Mary to tell her that she would conceive and give birth to a son who would be called the Son of God, Mary questioned the angel by saying, **"How shall this be, seeing I know not a man?"** (Luke 1:34). In other words, there was no physical, human seed for her to conceive because she had never been intimate with a man. Gabriel's answer reveals how the Word of God is the seed of life.

"And the angel answered and said unto her, The Holy Ghost shall come upon [you], and the power of the Highest shall overshadow [you]: therefore also that holy thing which shall be born of [you] shall be called the Son of God."

Luke 1:35

"And Mary said, Behold the handmaid of the Lord; be it unto me according to [Your] word. . . ."

Luke 1:38

In the scriptures recorded in Genesis, chapter 1, and here in the gospel of Luke, we see two examples of the creative power of the Word of God. In Genesis the Spirit of God moved upon the face of the waters as God spoke, saying, "Let there be" and there was. Here in Luke's gospel, we see the angel explaining to Mary how she would conceive a baby who is God's Son, and He would be called the Word of God. The Spirit of God would move upon her and would deposit that seed of the spoken Word, which Mary readily received (**"Be it unto me according to [Your] word . . . "**). That spoken Word of God, presented to Mary by the power of the Holy Spirit, brought forth Jesus, the living Word of God.

> **"And the Word was made flesh, and dwelt among us, (and we beheld his glory, the glory as of the only begotten of the Father,) full of grace and truth."**
> **John 1:14**

Could Mary have refused the will of God and told the angel that she wasn't interested in God's offer for her to be the mother of Jesus? Yes, for God has given all of mankind the authority to choose. God gave man dominion over His creation and the ability to obey or disobey His will. If Mary had refused, God would have had to find someone else, but Mary chose to receive the Word of God. By receiving the Word the angel brought to her, she physically conceived the seed of God's Word that produced a baby.

Who was this baby that was born to Mary, and why was He different than any other man?

Chapter 5

A BETTER SACRIFICE

We have already seen that all of mankind was born of the seed of Adam, and as a result, all have received Adam's sinful nature. Jesus was not born of the seed of man, and therefore did not receive Adam's sinful nature, but the nature of the seed from which He was born. Jesus was therefore called the "second man," that is, the second man who was actually made in the image of God as Adam was before he sinned.

In the Book of Hebrews Jesus is described as **"Being the brightness of his** (God's) **glory, and the express image of his** (God's) **person . . ." (Hebrews 1:3).**

Jesus was the perfect image and likeness of God the Father. When Philip asked Jesus to show him and the other disciples the Father, Jesus replied by saying, **"Have I been among you all this time and you do not know me, Philip? The one who has seen me has seen the Father . . ." (John 14:9 CSB).** And in chapter 10 Jesus says, **"I and my Father are one" (John 10:30).**

But how can Jesus be just like God the Father and yet be born a man? When Paul writes to the church at Philippi, he describes Jesus before His birth.

"Who, being in the form of God, thought it not robbery to be equal with God: But made himself of no reputation, and took upon him the form of a servant, and was made in the likeness of men."
Philippians 2:6,7

The *New Living Translation* words this portion of scripture like this:

"Though he was God, he did not think of equality with God as something to cling to. Instead, he gave up his divine privileges; he took the humble position of a slave and was born as a human being. . . ."

From these scriptures we see that before Jesus was born as a baby to Mary, He was equal with God and indeed was God. The Bible describes God as a Trinity. The idea of a "Trinity" is hard for man to understand. Though the word "Trinity" does not appear in scripture, it describes the relationship between God the Father, God the Son and God the Holy Spirit. This is not three separate Gods, but three individual expressions of the one true and living God who is uniquely and perfectly represented in three persons.

This is readily seen at the baptism of Jesus where the Spirit descends and remains upon Jesus as He is in the waters of the Jordan River, while at the same time God speaks from Heaven saying: **"This is my beloved Son, in whom I am well pleased"** **(Matthew 3:17).** The Son of God is in the river, the Spirit of God is visibly descending upon Him and God the Father speaks from Heaven. Also, in the epistle of John, the Trinity is described: **"For there are three that bear record in heaven, the Father, the Word, and the Holy Ghost: and these three are one"** (1 John 5:7).

Here the Son of God is referred to as the Word. We have already looked at the times Jesus is called the Word of God. In Paul's letter to the Ephesians he plainly says that God **". . . created all things by Jesus Christ" (Ephesians 3:9).** God spoke the Word, and all of creation came into being. It was this same Word that was in the beginning with God and was God (John 1:1) that became the seed that Mary received, and Jesus was born a man.

The scriptures already cited should answer anyone's question as to whether Jesus was deity (God) or not. Jesus declared His relationship with God the Father before His birth in that manger in Bethlehem when He was confronting the religious leaders. Jesus said:

". . . If God were your Father, [you] would love me: for I proceeded forth and came from God; neither came I of myself, but he sent me."

John 8:42

Again, Jesus said:

"Your father Abraham rejoiced to see my day: and he saw it and was glad. Then said the Jews unto him, [You] are not yet fifty years old, and [have you] seen Abraham? Jesus said unto them, Verily, verily, I say unto you, Before Abraham was, I am."

John 8:56-58

And then again, Jesus declared as He is in prayer:

"And now, O Father, glorify Me with Yourself, with the glory which I had with You before the world was"
(John 17:5 NKJV).

These scriptures reveal the deity of Jesus and His work in creation and eternal existence, but why did He need to become a man?

First, we understand that God created all things and then gave to man authority and dominion over all of His creation.

"And God said, Let us make man in our image, after our likeness: and let them have dominion over . . . all the earth . . . ."
Genesis 1:26

The Book of Psalms declares the same thing:

"When I consider Your heavens, the work of Your fingers, the moon and the stars, which You have ordained; what is man that You take thought of him, and the son of man that You care for him? Yet You have made him a little lower than God, and You crown him with glory and majesty! You make him to rule over the works of Your hands; You have put all things under his feet."
Psalm 8:3-6 NASB

"The heaven, even the heavens, are the LORD's: but the earth [has] he given to the children of men."
Psalm 115:16

The reason God needed to become a man was because God had given authority and dominion unto man.

"For as the Father has life in Himself; so He has granted to the Son to have life in Himself, and has given Him authority to execute judgment also, because He is the Son of Man."

John 5:26,27 NKJV

Notice, it does not say because Jesus was the "Son of God," but the "Son of Man." The first reason God had to become a man was because God had given to man dominion and authority over the earth.

The second reason was man's need for a perfect, sinless man who was able to live a life free from sin and to perfectly keep and obey all of the righteous commandments of God.

Man was incapable of living a sinless life because of his sinful nature he inherited from his father Adam. Jesus was not born of Adam's seed, but the perfect, incorruptible seed of God's Word (1 Peter 1:23).

We have already seen in previous chapters how the animal sacrifices of the Old Testament were substitutes for receiving the judgments of man's sin. The one who sinned and broke the law of God was under the judgment of death, but he could bring to the priest a sacrifice. The sacrifice was a certain kind of animal that had no blemishes of any kind. The one bringing the sacrifice would lay his hands on the head of the animal and by faith transfer his guilt and sin to the animal, which was then slain. The required judgment of death was fulfilled, and the man was delivered from the judgment of death for his sin.

The Bible says, **"For *it is* not possible that the blood of bulls and goats could take away sins" (Hebrews 10:4 NKJV).** The animal received the judgment of death for the man's sin, but that animal could never give the man righteousness. It could not take away the old, sinful nature man had inherited from his father's seed. Man's need of righteousness could not be achieved by man's own efforts, which were always flawed because of his flawed nature.

Mankind needed someone else to accomplish what he was not capable of doing for himself. Humanity needed someone who was qualified to stand before God without being guilty of sin, someone who had lived a righteous, holy and sinless life, perfectly fulfilling all God required; and that person had to be a man—a man who was willing to live his life as a substitute; i.e., making his righteousness (rightness or sinless life) available for others to receive.

This man had to also be willing to take upon himself the judgment of God for man's sin. When a person sinned and disobeyed a commandment of God, he could bring a sacrifice to be his substitute in judgment. This substitute needed to be qualified first of all as being worthy by having no observable blemish. In the Old Testament, the substitute (the animal) was thoroughly examined by the priest. The person bringing the sacrifice was not examined, but the sacrifice (the animal) was what was examined to be a worthy substitute.

Jesus was the only man who qualified as our substitute. He was the only One born with a sinless nature and possessed the very nature, image and likeness of God. No one else qualified to give us righteousness because no one else possessed God's righteousness to give.

The last night Jesus spent with His disciples was the night of the preparation for the Jewish Passover. The Passover Feast was celebrated yearly and was instituted by God as a requirement for the entire nation of Israel to observe. This feast commemorated the final judgment on the nation of Egypt who had enslaved the Israelites. Because the Jews lived among the Egyptians, the judgment of God on Egypt would have been experienced by the Jews also unless there was a way to protect Israel from this judgment.

God instructed Moses to command all of Israel to take a lamb and to kill it and smear its blood on the entrance to their homes. They were then required to roast the lamb and to eat it. The judgment that followed was the death of the firstborn son of every family. Every household who refused to kill and eat the sacrifice, protecting the entrance to their dwelling with the blood of the lamb, experienced the death of their firstborn in that house whether the firstborn was the father or the son of that family.

At that time neither the Israelites nor the Egyptians would have understood the significance of this command of God beyond the immediate application to their day. The only thing they would have understood was that every household where the blood of the lamb was applied to the door and the lamb itself had been received as a meal was protected, but those who had not dealt with the lamb experienced death.

We now understand that the significance of this Passover Feast illustrates far more than Israel's deliverance from Egyptian slavery. The firstborn son represents Adam and all of his descendants who are under the judgment of death unless they partake of God's substitute, Jesus, **"the Lamb of God** which [takes] **away the sin of the world" (John 1:29).**

On the night Jesus ate that final Passover meal, He took bread and broke it and gave to His disciples, and said, "... **Take, eat; this is my body" (Matthew 26:26),** and taking the cup of wine, He said, "... **Drink ... all of it; for this is my blood of the new testament, which is shed for many for the remission of sins" (Matthew 26:27-28).**

Jesus was declaring the end of the Old Testament and the beginning of the New. The fulfillment of that first prophetic word to Adam and Eve in the garden had taken place. The "seed of the woman" had arrived and becoming a man lived a sinless life, perfectly righteous in God's eyes. Jesus was the perfect substitute, taking sinful man's place and the perfect sacrifice taking God's judgment for man. When Jesus told His disciples to receive the broken bread as His body and the cup of wine as His blood, He was declaring the end of an old system that could never make man righteous or remove his guilt. Man could now become righteous before God by receiving the righteousness Jesus possessed as a free gift. Mankind would no longer be required to live with the constant reminder of his sin, but could now live with an understanding that his sin and the law that required his death were both nailed to the cross of Christ Jesus (Colossians 2:14).

Jesus, "the seed of the woman," would first be bruised as part of the work necessary to "bruise" (crush) the serpent's head. Jesus had to be "bruised" to destroy the serpent that had deceived man and brought him into the slavery of sin and death.

This imagery depicts a poisonous snake that has bitten all of mankind. All have been infected with the venom of sin that has released in man the certainty of death. But then a man appears who has not had this fatal bite and is willing to take all the venom this serpent has. This unselfish act of love would cost this man His life as He would receive the venom, but simultaneously would crush the head of the serpent with His wounded heel. The "anti-venom," so to speak, would then be made available to whoever is willing to receive it.

The "bruise" Jesus received was, in fact, the entire curse Adam had released into the earth. This "bruise" is exemplified by the crown of thorns on Jesus' head and the beatings He received by the Roman soldiers and ultimately the cross upon which He was crucified.

There are many Old Testament examples illustrated by Jesus' redemptive work. The crown of thorns on Jesus' head that pierced His brow and shed His blood was payment for the curse spoken over Adam after his sin.

". . . Cursed is the ground because of you . . . It will produce thorns for you . . . by the sweat of your brow you will eat your food. . . ."
Genesis 3:17-19 NIV

The cross upon which Jesus was crucified reveals the place where Jesus bore the entire curse produced by man's sin.

"Christ [has] redeemed us from the curse of the law, being made a curse for us: for it is written, Cursed is every one that [hangs] on a tree."
Galatians 3:13

The curse listed in the Book of Leviticus, chapter 26, and in the Book of Deuteronomy, chapter 28, shows us what Jesus experienced for our deliverance. Every kind of sickness and disease, condition of poverty and the fear and torment they produce were placed upon Him on the cross.

"As Moses lifted up the serpent in the wilderness, even so must the Son of man be lifted up."

John 3:14

When the people of Israel disobeyed the commandments of God, serpents came into the desert and bit many of them. Many people were dying from the serpent's venomous bite. When Moses sought for a remedy, God told him to make a brazen serpent and put it on a pole in the midst of the camp. When anyone was bitten, if they would look upon the brazen serpent, they would be healed·

As the serpent was lifted up on the pole, Christ was lifted up on the cross. As the Israelites looked upon the serpent on the pole and were saved from death of the venomous bite of the serpent, so as anyone looks upon Jesus on the cross, they are saved from the resulting death from the fatal bite of sin. For our sin was lifted up on the cross as Jesus became sin for us (in our place, as our substitute).

"For He made Him who knew no sin to be sin for us, that we might become the righteousness of God in Him."

2 Corinthians 5:21 NKJV

Chapter 6

Jesus Is Man's Only Savior

There is a great emphasis today in our society for tolerance and coexistence for all people to get along with one another and to be accepting of different religions, philosophies and ideas. The idea of "only one way" to Heaven is criticized, and those who hold such exclusive ideas are labeled as ignorant or self-righteous and exclusive or even mean-spirited and dangerous to a peaceful society. But, the truth as expressed in the scriptures and experienced by millions of people, is condensed in a single statement of Jesus:

> **". . . I am the way, the truth, and the life: no man [comes] unto the Father, but by me."**
>
> **John 14:6**

There is no other religious leader, no other philosophy of man or founder of some religious sect who could ever qualify as the Savior of mankind. No one else has been born of a virgin or demonstrated the very character and nature of a loving God who is described as a Father who is in love with mankind. No one else has ever willingly given his life as a sacrifice to pay for man's sin. And certainly no one else has ever risen from the dead to show his victory over death and the wicked one he came to defeat.

Instead, most of the gods of other religions are angry tyrants who must be appeased by man's sacrifice or they require man to qualify himself, that is, to make himself acceptable by his own self efforts.

Only in Christ Jesus are people judged by what Jesus did for them and not what they can do for themselves. Forgiveness of sins and a restored fellowship with God are imparted to the one who knows he is incapable of saving himself and simply calls on God to forgive, cleanse and restore him because he places his trust in Christ and confesses Him as Lord.

If Jesus crushed the head of the serpent, the devil, why is the devil giving me such a bad time?

The following scriptures state Jesus' victory over the devil and his wicked works:

"Now is the judgment of this world: now shall the prince of this world be cast out."

John 12:31

"Forasmuch then as the children are partakers of flesh and blood, he also himself likewise took part of the same; that through death he might destroy him that had the power of death, that is, the devil; and

deliver them who through fear of death were all their lifetime subject to bondage."

Hebrews 2:14,15

"... For this purpose the Son of God was manifested, that he might destroy the works of the devil."

1 John 3:8

If the devil's works were destroyed by Jesus and those works are described as "killing, stealing and destroying" (John 10:10) and Jesus destroyed the power of sin, the power of death and the devil who had that power, how come there is so much sin and death still around?

To answer this question let's look at some of these scriptures more closely.

In Hebrews 2:14 the English words here are translated from the Greek language. This verse states that Jesus, through His death, might "destroy" him who had the "power" of death, that is, the devil. The word "destroy" here means "to render entirely idle, useless or unemployed" and the word "power" is the Greek word usually translated as "dominion." In other words, Jesus, through His death and resurrection, rendered the devil, whose dominion was death, "unemployed." Jesus, through the shedding of His blood, His death on the cross and His victory over death by His resurrection, cast the devil out of his position **("... Now shall the prince of this world be cast out" (John 12:31)** of ruling over man and subjecting him to the bondage of the fear of death (Hebrews 2:15).

The devil has not been annihilated, but he has been bound from ruling over those who come to Jesus and are spiritually born.

Many of the New Testament scriptures remind us that we are in a war and we have an enemy. Our enemy is not people, but our enemy is the devil and a host of wicked spirits.

"For we wrestle not against flesh and blood, but against principalities, against powers, against the rulers of the darkness of this world, against spiritual wickedness in high places."

Ephesians 6:12

We are told to be watchful, because we have an adversary who walks about seeking someone to destroy.

"Be sober, be vigilant; because your adversary, the devil. . . [walks] about, seeking whom he may devour."

1 Peter 5:8

You might notice in this scripture that the devil cannot just randomly devour or destroy whomever he wants. No, he must find someone who will employ him in his work of death and destruction. That is why we are told to recognize him and resist him. Jesus told His disciples:

"Behold, I give unto you power to tread on serpents and scorpions, and over all the power of the enemy: and nothing shall by any means hurt you."

Luke 10:19

Power, or actually the word here is "authority," is given to Jesus' disciples to tread on, metaphorically that is, to have authority over the devil and his works. That is why Jesus said after His resurrection, that He had all authority in Heaven and in earth and therefore gave us authority to go into the entire world and preach the gospel (Matthew 28:18,19). We are to cast out demons and bind up the work of the devil by the authority that has been given to us in the name of Jesus.

Many would say, "That sounds good, but in reality, why are so many Christians living a life of defeat and bound by fear? Where is the abundant life Jesus promised?"

The scriptures are full of admonitions to believers to be watchful, to be diligent in their resistance against the devices of the devil. We are told to be strong in the Lord and in the power of His might. We are to put on the armor of God so we will be able to stand against every work of darkness (Ephesians 6:10).

Just because the devil was defeated doesn't mean he is not actively working to oppose the plan of God. He is called "**the prince of the power of the air, the spirit that now** [works] **in the children of disobedience" (Ephesians 2:2).** He has a kingdom called the kingdom of darkness, and he is very busy deceiving mankind, bringing death and destruction into their lives and then blaming God for the results.

Some people would ask, "How can that be if Jesus truly defeated the devil?" Remember, Jesus rendered the devil idle, useless and unemployed. This is true for every believer who will resist the devil by submitting themselves to the Lord and standing strong in the armor of God, fighting in this spiritual battle. Jesus did not say that we would not be bothered by or encounter trouble. On the contrary, Jesus said, **"In the world you will have tribulation** (trouble)**; but be of good cheer, I have overcome the world" (John 16:33 NKJV).**

Why will we have trouble in the world? Because we are not of this world. The world is not referring to the planet earth, but the system of operation; that is, how things function and operate in the world. This world (its system of operation and how it functions) is not yet under the dominion and control of the Lord. Jesus said, **". . . My kingdom is not of this world . . ." (John 18:36)**. To believers, the Word of God declares, **"For he has rescued us from the kingdom of darkness and transferred us into the kingdom of his dear Son" (Colossians 1:13 NLT)**. We are living in this world, but we are not of this world's system of operation, which is under the control of the devil.

When Jesus was confronted by the devil in the wilderness, the scriptures say that the devil tempted Him by showing Him the kingdoms of this world and promised to give Jesus these kingdoms.

> **"Then the devil, taking Him up on a high mountain, showed Him all the kingdoms of the world . . . And the devil said . . . All this authority I will give You, and their glory; for this has been delivered to me, and I give it to whomever I wish."**
>
> **Luke 4:5,6 NKJV**

The Bible says that this was a real temptation. Did the devil have authority over the kingdoms of this world? Apparently so, for he said, **"For this has been delivered to me."** Who do you think gave that authority to the devil? It certainly was not God. God had given man authority and dominion. The psalmist said, **"The heaven, even the heavens, are the Lord's: but the earth [has] he given to the children of men" (Psalm 115:16)**. How did man give the devil his authority? It says in Romans 6:16, **"Know [you] not, that to whom [you] yield yourselves servants to obey, his servants [you] are to whom [you] obey; whether of sin unto death, or of obedience unto righteousness?"**

Then in Romans 5:17 it says, **"For if by one man's offence death reigned by one. . . ."** The one who committed the offence for death to reign was Adam, and by his sin he submitted himself as a servant to the one he obeyed and that was the devil. Adam was the one who delivered the authority and dominion God had given him over to the devil. Ever since that time the devil has had dominion over the kingdoms of this world.

The Bible gives many examples regarding the kingdoms of this world and who rules them. There may be a man on the throne of a physical kingdom, but the Bible reveals that behind the earthly ruler is an unseen demonic ruler, a spirit that attempts to control the functions of that kingdom.

Chapter 7

AN INVISIBLE KINGDOM

In the Book of Daniel, we find that behind the human ruler of a kingdom there is another ruler who functions in that kingdom in the spiritual realm. Daniel is a prophet of God and is living in Persia. While he is praying, he has an angelic visitation. The angel tells him that he was sent from the throne of God with a message for Daniel from the very first day he had prayed, but this angel was hindered from bringing Daniel the message because of one who is called the prince of the kingdom of Persia. After delivering the message of God to Daniel, he says, **". . . now will I return to fight with the prince of Persia: and when I am gone forth, lo, the prince of Grecia shall come" (Daniel 10:20).**

Although the angel that came to Daniel was not named in this passage of scripture, we can assume it was Gabriel who had previously come to Daniel as is described in both chapters 8 and 9 of the Book of Daniel. This angel was hindered for 21 days by one named the prince of the kingdom of Persia. At that time Daniel was one of the officials in the kingdom of

Persia under Cyrus the king. Obviously, it was not King Cyrus who was able to detain the angel Gabriel from reaching Daniel, but an unseen ruler called a prince who ruled over the spiritual realm of this physical kingdom.

Also, this angel told Daniel that he was going to return to fight with the prince of Persia, and afterward the prince of Grecia would come. Historically, we know that the Greeks defeated the Persians. Revealed in this scripture is that every kingdom of man is mirrored by a spiritual kingdom and king. A man could not hinder or defeat the angel of God, but a spiritual prince or ruler who opposed the angel of God hindered him.

This same idea is seen in the Book of Ezekiel, chapter 28 and verse 1. The Word of the Lord comes to the prophet addressing the "prince of Tyrus." This man is the ruler of the island fortress of Tyrus. With its double walls 150 foot high and a powerful Navy, this city was thought to be impossible to conquer. The city was extremely wealthy because of its vast commerce from far away lands. It had an abundance of silver and gold.

All of these things caused the ruler, "the prince of Tyrus," to be prideful to the place that his "heart was lifted up because of his riches." God describes the condition of this man's heart: **"You have said, 'I am a God, I sit in the seat of God, in the midst of the seas; yet** [you] **are a man, and not God, though** [you] **set** [your] **heart as the heart of God"** (Ezekiel 28:2). God continues to speak of the pending judgment that would fall on this city and its prince.

In the same chapter this prophetic word, addressing the prince of Tyrus, is followed by another word addressing the king of Tyrus. This "king" of Tyrus is obviously someone different than the prince, for he is described as one who had been in the Eden of God and who had been upon the holy mountain of God. This "king" is called "the anointed cherub that covers." We see that this one was at one time perfect in all his ways until iniquity was found in him. (See Ezekiel 28:15.) This "king" was Lucifer who was cast out of Heaven. He was ruling behind the scenes of the earthly kingdom in a spiritual kingdom, and the man on the throne in Tyrus held the same characteristics as this wicked, spiritual ruler.

It was also in the Book of Daniel that a vision or dream was given to King Nebuchadnezzar that Daniel interpreted. In this dream, all the kingdoms of the world were represented by a great image of a man. The head, the shoulders and arms, the belly and thighs, and then the legs and feet each represented the primary kingdoms from Daniel's day to the coming of Christ.

In the dream there was a stone that fell on the feet of this image, and when it did the whole image was shattered and became a pile of dust that the wind blew away. Then that stone grew until it filled the entire earth. The parts of the image represented all the kingdoms of the world, and the stone represented Christ who is the "stone the builders rejected" and "the foundation stone of the Church" and the "headstone of the corner" described in many scriptures. Christ came to establish an everlasting Kingdom that will fill all the earth.

The good news is that one day, ". . . **The kingdoms of this world are become the kingdoms of our Lord, and of his Christ; and he shall reign for ever and ever" (Revelation 11:15).**

It is exciting to think that we have a part in taking the Kingdom of God to all the earth, bringing the good news to people

61

and seeing them delivered out of one kingdom and brought into the Kingdom of God (Colossians 1:13).

The stone that crushed the great image that represented the kingdoms of the world began small but grew until it had filled all the earth. This stone is the Kingdom of God, and it came to the earth when Jesus was born.

"And, behold, [you shall] conceive in [your] womb, and bring forth a son, and [shall] call his name JESUS. He shall be great, and shall be called the Son of the Highest: and the Lord God shall give unto him the throne of his father David: And he shall reign over the house of Jacob for ever; and of his kingdom there shall be no end."

Luke 1:31-33

Jesus was born to be a King; however, His Kingdom is not of this world.

Jesus answered, "My kingdom is not of this world . . . but now My kingdom is not from here."

John 18:36 NKJV

Everything Jesus did and taught gave demonstration to the nature of His Kingdom. When Jesus went to Galilee, He preached to the people there about His Kingdom.

. . . Jesus came to Galilee, preaching the gospel of the kingdom of God, and saying, "The time is fulfilled, and the kingdom of God is at hand. Repent, and believe the gospel."

Mark 1:14,15 NKJV

"But if I cast out demons by the Spirit of God, surely the kingdom of God has come upon you."

Matthew 12:28 NKJV

Jesus declared the gospel (good news) and demonstrated the power of His Kingdom by destroying the works of the kingdom of darkness. Matthew's gospel describes the works Jesus did.

"And great multitudes came unto him, having with them those that were lame, blind, dumb, maimed, and many others, and cast them down at Jesus' feet; and he healed them: insomuch that the multitude wondered, when they saw the dumb to speak, the maimed to be whole, the lame to walk and the blind to see: and they glorified the God of Israel."

Matthew 15:30,31

Chapter 8

AMBASSADORS OF HEAVEN

God has a plan to cover the earth with His glory and to bring all of the kingdoms of this world under the dominion of the Kingdom of God (Habakkuk 2:14; Revelation 11:15). We find in the Book of Acts a clue regarding the coming of the Lord.

> **"And he will send you Jesus, the Messiah, the chosen one for you. For he must remain in heaven until the restoration of all things has taken place, *fulfilling everything that God said* long ago through his holy prophets."**
>
> **Acts 3:20,21** TPT

In Acts 1:9 Jesus ascends into Heaven after His resurrection, but not before He commissioned His disciples to carry the gospel to all the nations of the earth (Matthew 28:18-20). Believers were to begin in the city of Jerusalem and then go to all of Judea, then Samaria, and then to **"the uttermost part of the earth" (Acts 1:8)**.

The Kingdom of God was not of this world, but as people hear the gospel and believe and receive Jesus as Lord, they are delivered out of the spiritual kingdom of darkness and are brought into the Kingdom of God (Colossians 1:13). The stone (Jesus) that fell upon and destroyed the image (all the kingdoms of this world) began to grow until it filled all the earth (Daniel 2:35).

When people hear and believe the gospel, they still live in the same geographical location and in the same nation or kingdom of the earth on the outside, but inside they belong to the Kingdom of God. When Jesus was asked about the Kingdom of God He said,

". . . The kingdom of God does not come with observation; nor will they say, 'See here!' or 'See there!' For indeed, the kingdom of God is within you"
(Luke 17:20,21 NKJV).

As people live as citizens of the Kingdom of God on the inside, they become ambassadors for Christ to the world around them (2 Corinthians 5:19,20). Believers are to influence and transform their neighborhoods and communities, spreading the Kingdom from person to person until entire nations come to the Lord.

The prophet Isaiah spoke of this time when believers are carrying the light of God's glory and those who are in darkness will see the light and turn to the Lord:

"Nations will come to your light, and kings to the brightness of your rising."

Isaiah 60:3 AMP

When will Jesus return? When the Church (all believers) have fulfilled their commission of covering the earth with the glory of God as the waters cover the sea (Isaiah 11:9; Habakkuk 2:14). What an awesome responsibility the Lord has given us. It is a good thing He has equipped us to accomplish the task.

"But you shall receive power when the Holy Spirit has come upon you; and you shall be witnesses to Me. . . ."

Acts 1:8 NKJV

Jesus' command to His disciples was to carry the gospel to the ends of the earth, but not in their own strength. They were to wait for the coming of the Holy Spirit to fill them and equip them for the job.

On the Day of Pentecost, the Holy Spirit came upon one hundred and twenty of them as they waited in an upper room in the city of Jerusalem (Acts 2:1,2). They were filled with the Holy Spirit and spoke in tongues and prophesied, resulting in Peter preaching to the crowds in the streets and 3,000 people believed and were brought into the Kingdom of God that day.

Over and over again throughout the book of Acts, believers prayed and then were filled with the Holy Spirit and spoke the Word of God with boldness. Multitudes heard and believed and rejoiced in being born again and filled with the Holy Spirit.

Paul traveled to the city of Ephesus and met twelve men and asked them, **"Did you receive the Holy Spirit when you believed?" (Acts 19:2 NKJV).** Upon further questioning,

Paul finds out that these men had never heard about the Holy Spirit and were only familiar with what John the Baptist had preached. Paul instructed them that John had preached about the coming of Christ, but now Christ had come and fulfilled the work of salvation that they should receive. These twelve men believed and received Jesus as Savior and Lord and were baptized in water. Then Paul laid his hands on them, and they were filled with the Holy Spirit. These men were now equipped to carry the gospel of Jesus with the power of God.

My Personal Testimony

My personal testimony began when I was twelve years old. My family did not go to church, but my parents loved to watch Billy Graham crusades on television.

One day I came into the house from being outside and as I walked through the living room, Billy Graham was preaching and I heard him say something like, "You must be born again. You must ask Jesus into your life and be forgiven of your sins." I did not know what all of that meant, but by the time I got to my bedroom, I felt a conviction that I had never asked Jesus into my life. Falling on my knees next to my bed, I prayed some simple prayer asking Jesus to forgive me and come into my life. I did not know then what had taken place. Seemingly nothing was different, but I felt like I had done something important.

Shortly after that, I found a Gideon New Testament I had been given at school and started reading the Bible. A few months later, I had a desire to go to church and learn about God. I went to a church and got baptized in water, but I never really learned about God's plan for my life beyond just trying to be good and not sin. Although I did not think I was wicked, I did know that my life choices did not always please God. I would go to church and "repent" before God and try to do better, but my life was a series of bad choices, repenting, trying to do better, failing and repenting again. I was a not-so-victorious Christian.

After several years of marriage, my wife began to hunger after the things of God and was baptized in the Holy Spirit. Initially, I was not happy with her newfound love for God because it put a spotlight on my halfhearted and lukewarm commitment to God.

Attempting to satisfy my wife and parents, who were attending a small church near where I had grown up, I began to go to church each week and a new hunger began to grow in me as I heard things about God I never knew. God loved me more than I could ever imagine, and His plan for my life was not limited to a set of rules of do's and don'ts. But He wanted to fill my life with every good thing and deposit His Kingdom and power inside of me in the person of the Holy Spirit.

After several months I went to the altar after a morning service and prayed to receive the baptism in the Holy Spirit. My life changed radically, and this experience set me on the most wonderful journey of my life.

I have not been exempt from trials, troubles and problems, but God's grace has also been there to help me in difficult times and bring me to a place of victory.

Three Questions for You

I have three questions for you today:

Question #1: Have you ever been born again?

We have looked at God's original purpose for man to live as God's image and likeness, ruling in life to accomplish God's will. Because sin was an inheritance none of us could avoid, we needed a Savior to deliver us out of the kingdom of darkness (sin) and to be born again into a new family, not just being forgiven of sin, but being transformed on the inside, receiving a new nature. The only way that can happen is to go to Jesus, man's only Savior, and ask Him to do for us what we cannot do for ourselves.

Here is a sample prayer you might pray to receive God's forgiveness and transforming work:

"God, I call upon the name of Your Son, Jesus Christ, today, asking You to forgive me of all sin and change my nature to be born again of Your Spirit. I believe that Jesus is the Son of God and was born as a man and lived a perfect and sinless life according to Your perfect law. I believe Jesus died for me, and the judgment of all my sin was placed upon Him. I believe Jesus arose from the grave victorious over death, ascended into heaven and sits at the right hand of God the Father. This day I confess that Jesus Christ is my Lord and Savior. I thank You for forgiving me of all sin and for giving me a new life that I receive now, in Jesus' name."

Question #2: Have you been baptized with the Holy Spirit?

There are many people who would say that they received the Holy Spirit when they were born again, and I agree. The scriptures show us that the Holy Spirit literally enters our physical body and gives new life to our spirit man. We are changed because the Holy Spirit has arrived and lives in us (Romans 8:9). But there is a subsequent experience to being born again by the Holy Spirit that brings the power of God into your life, equipping you to do what God has called you to do.

After Jesus was resurrected He came to His disciples and breathed on them, saying, **"Receive the Holy Spirit" (John 20:22 NKJV),** but right after that He told them to wait for the coming of the Holy Spirit so they would be empowered to do the work of the ministry (Acts 1:4). Although Jesus had breathed on them to receive the Spirit, He commanded them to wait, and ten days later they were all filled with the Holy Spirit (Acts 2:4).

Several years later Philip left Jerusalem and went to the city of Samaria and preached the gospel to the people there. " . . . **When they believed Philip preaching the things concerning the kingdom of God, and the name of Jesus Christ, they were baptized, both men and women"** (Acts 8:12).

Sometime later the apostles at Jerusalem heard that the people of Samaria had received the Word of God, and they sent Peter and John to them. When they arrived, they ". . . **prayed for them that they might receive the Holy Spirit. For as yet He had fallen upon none of them. They had only been baptized in the name of the Lord Jesus. Then they laid hands on them, and they received the Holy Spirit"** (Acts 8:15-17 NKJV).

These new believers received the baptism in the Holy Spirit, who empowered them to do the things God had called them to do in His power, not in their own power.

A common problem in the church today is that people may have had an experience like this with God five, ten, twenty or more years ago, but they live an unsuccessful Christian life that is devoid of God's power or presence. The Bible urges us to not only receive the baptism in the Holy Spirit, but to continuously be filled with Him (Ephesians 5:18). The Lord has called us to lay down our lives by giving demonstration to His life in us, and that starts with being filled with His Holy Spirit.

Here is a simple prayer you might pray as an example of asking God to fill you with the Holy Spirit:

"Lord Jesus, the scriptures say that John the Baptist baptized people in water, but You would baptize us in the Holy Spirit. I know I need the power of the Holy Spirit to work in my life so I can do the things You have called me to do, not in my power but in Yours. I yield myself to You now and ask You to fill me with the Holy Spirit. I yield all of me to You now and thank You for filling me with the Spirit of God that I receive now in Jesus' name, Amen."

Question # 3: Do you know what God has called you to do?

God's will is not a mystery. The scriptures tell us plainly that God wants to bless us, prosper us, give us the desires of our heart and help us to live in peace. God wants us to be fruitful in every good thing and to live a life that is rich in the love of God and to fulfill all of our days with joy. But how we fit into God's plan and His unique and distinctive purpose for us individually is sometimes less obvious. So, regardless of how long we have walked with the Lord, whether a few days or many years, finding out His specific will for us personally is something we should all seek to know and understand.

Where do we begin? We begin by doing the things God has instructed all of us to do and to do those things faithfully. Here is a list of some of those most obvious things:

Pray – Prayer is not optional, and many believers do not practice praying scriptural prayers. Many people pray, even those who don't really know God, but they pray prayers of desperation or deal making with God. Oftentimes they are trying to get God to do something for them by begging or pleading, hoping God will show them pity and answer their prayer. But praying according to the Word of God is not bombarding Heaven with desperate cries for help, but aligning ourselves with Heaven to pray for God's will to be done.

Jesus taught the disciples to pray, declaring, **"Your kingdom come, Your will be done on earth as it is in Heaven" (Matthew 6:10 NKJV).** God's will for you is always good, so asking God to reveal His will to you is according to His plan. Ask God now to show you how He wants to use you for His glory and your good.

Church – The Church is not a building or location, but the Church is the gathering together of believers. The Greek word translated Church in English means an assembly. The Church is not a random pile of parts, but a purposeful assembly of different parts fitly joined together (Ephesians 2:21). The Church is described as the human body with many individual parts and purposes that all work together for the body to live and function in a healthy manner (1 Corinthians 12:14-27).

The Church is also described as a building with many parts uniquely joined together for a perfect fit. Walls, roof, flooring and foundation are all parts of the same building, but each is designed to fulfill a particular purpose and function.

The Bible admonishes the members of the Church to not forsake the assembling together (Hebrews 10:25). When we come together, we are to each bring with us the gifting of God within us to share with others what we have and to receive from them what they have so we may all be made stronger and better together.

It is often in times of worship, prayer or preaching of the Word of God that God touches our hearts and gives us instructions for our lives.

Serving – We have been called of God to serve one another. Jesus said if we save our lives, we will lose them, but if we lose our lives, we will save them (Matthew 16:25). Jesus did not come to be served but to serve, and we are called to do the same. Laying down your life for someone else is not usually referring to dying physically for another, but laying aside your comfort and convenience to help someone else.

When the disciples were arguing which one would be the greatest, Jesus did not rebuke them. He simply got up from the table, girded Himself with a towel, got a basin of water and began washing the feet of His disciples. They were all amazed that He, their Lord, would literally stoop to do such a menial task, for that was the job of the lowest servant.

Having completed the task, Jesus sat down and said to them, **"Do you know what I have done to you? You call Me Teacher and Lord, and you say well, for so I am. If I then, your Lord and Teacher, have washed your feet, you also ought to wash one another's feet. For I have given you an example, that you should do as I have done to you"** (John 13:12-15 NKJV).

In our modern world, we don't need to literally wash each other's feet to fulfill the command to serve one another. But, if we would prefer others ahead of ourselves and if we would purposefully look to see how we could help, bless and serve others as Jesus did, and do it, not for some self-seeking appreciation, but out of the love of God, we would be fulfilling God's purpose.

You may not know the ultimate purpose God has for your life right now, but if you are doing the things you know God has asked you to do, then He can direct you into that service you have been uniquely designed to accomplish. Preacher, schoolteacher, astronaut, banker, business executive, school board member or President, the list is endless, but the need is great. You may feel unqualified to do what God has purposed for you, but then that just makes you even more dependent on Him.

If you will just do what you know to do, then God will show you more perfectly His divine plan. Whatever your station in life may be right now, you have been called as an ambassador of Heaven, representing the King of kings and the Lord of lords on planet earth. Let us rule well and bring honor to His image.

Other books by Dr. Dan Coflin...

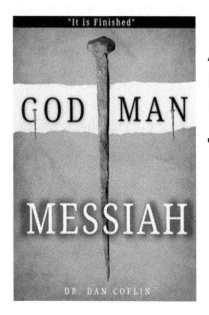

A study of the Gospels Revealing the Life, Ministry and Lordship of Jesus Christ of Nazareth

A daily devotional designed to gather together a busy family before each member hurries off to begin their day

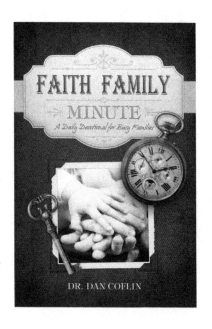

To place an order, please visit:
coflinpublishing.com

CPSIA information can be obtained
at www.ICGtesting.com
Printed in the USA
BVHW040435260422
635047BV00005B/16